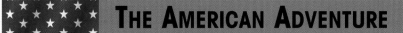

THE FIRST RAILROADS

SALLY SENZELL ISAACS

Heinemann Library
Chicago, Illinois

© 2004 Heinemann Library
a division of Reed Elsevier Inc.
Chicago, Illinois

Customer Service 888-454-2279

Visit our website at www.heinemannlibrary.com

Produced for Heinemann Library by
   Bender Richardson White.
Editor: Lionel Bender
Designer and Page Makeup: Ben White
Picture Researcher: Cathy Stastny
Production Controller: Kim Richardson

07 06 05 04 03
10 9 8 7 6 5 4 3 2 1

Printed in China, by WKT Company Limited

Library of Congress Cataloging-in-Publication Data.
Isaacs, Sally Senzell, 1950-
   The first railroads / Sally Senzell Isaacs.
      p. cm. – (The American adventure)
   Summary: An account of the early railroad era in the United
   States, describing the first trains, progress in train
   development, the growth of railroad networks, and the
   contribution of trains to the growth of the country.
   ISBN 1-4034-2506-X (library binding : alk. paper)
 - ISBN 1-4034-4791-8 (pbk. : alk. paper)
   1. Railroads–United States–History–Juvenile literature. 2.
   Railroads–Trains–Juvenile literature. 3. Locomotives—J
   Juvenile literature. [1. Railroads–History. 2. Railroads–Trains.
   3. Locomotives.] I. Title.
   HE2751.I8 2004
   385'.0973–dc22
                                              2003013022

Special thanks to Mike Carpenter and Geof Knight at Heinemann
Library for editorial and design guidance and direction.

Acknowledgments
The producers and publishers are grateful to the following for
permission to reproduce copyright material:
Bettmann/Corbis Images, page 10, 20.
Peter Newark's American Pictures, pages 6, 8, 11, 13, 15, 17,
19, 23, 24, 26.

Illustrations by Mark Bergin
Maps by Stefan Chabluk
Cover art by Mark Bergin

Every effort has been made to contact copyright holders of any
material reproduced in this book. Omissions will be rectified in
subsequent printings if notice is given to the publisher.

QUOTATIONS

The quotations in this book come from:

Bakeless, John (editor), *The Journals of Lewis and
Clark*. New York: Penguin Books U.S.A., Inc.,
1964.

Ambrose, Stephen E., *Undaunted Courage:
Meriwether Lewis, Thomas Jefferson, and the
Opening of the American West*. New York: Simon &
Schuster, 1995.

Ambrose, Stephen E., *Lewis and Clark Voyage of
Discovery*. Washington, D.C.: National Geographic
Society, 1998.

The Author
Sally Senzell Isaacs is a professional writer and
editor of nonfiction books for children. She
graduated from Indiana University, earning a B.S.
degree in education with majors in American
history and sociology. She is the author of the nine
titles in the *America in the Time of...* series
published by Heinemann Library and of the first
sixteen titles in Heinemann Library's *Picture the
Past* series. Sally Senzell Isaacs lives in New
Jersey with her husband and two children.

The Consultant
Our thanks to Dr. Richard Jensen, Professor
Emeritus of History at the University of Illinois, for
his assistance in the preparation of this book.

★★★ ABOUT THIS BOOK

This book is about America's first railroads. The term *America* means the United States of America (also called the U.S.) The term *railroad* refers to the tracks that trains travel on or to the trains, tracks, stations, and the people who manage them. The book covers the period from 1820 to 1890. This was a time of remarkable growth for the United States. Factories and businesses grew. So did the population. With this growth came a need for better transportation. The country's first trains came from England but U.S. engineers later made many railroad improvements. In most countries of the world today, the central government owns the railroads. In the United States, the railroads have always been privately owned but the federal government is responsible for creating safety laws and making decisions about routes and finances.

★★★ CONTENTS

ABOUT THE SERIES

The American Adventure is a series of books about important events that shaped the United States of America. Each book focuses on one event. While learning about the event, the reader will also learn how the people and places of the time period influenced the nation's future. The little illustrations at the top left of each two-page article are a symbol of the times. They are identified in the Contents on page 3.

▼ This map shows the United States today, with the borders and names of all the states. Refer to this map, or to the one on pages 28 and 29, to locate places talked about in this book.

AMERICA'S STORY

Throughout the book, the yellow panels, showing the luggage of a rail traveler, contain information that tells the more general history of the United States of America.

THE FEATURE STORY

The green panels, showing a steam locomotive, contain more detailed information about the first railroads in the United States, this book's feature story.

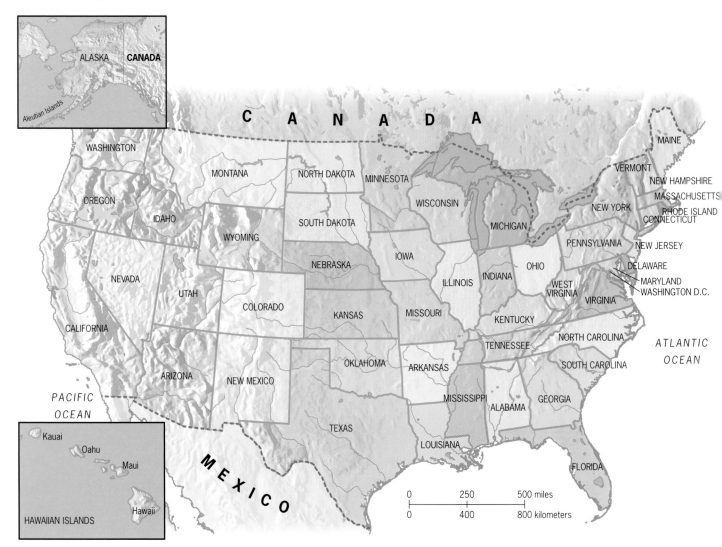

THE FIRST RAILROADS:
INTRODUCTION

Today people can travel from city to city in a few hours or less. Planes, trains, buses, and cars make the trip easy and comfortable. Transportation has changed greatly since the early days of the United States. In the early 1800s, a short journey could take several days. There were few roads between towns, and those roads were narrow and bumpy. To get from place to place, a person walked, rode a horse, or traveled by boat. When people needed to transport things, such as lumber or grain, they loaded a wagon and hitched up a horse or mule to pull it. Sometimes they used boats.

The nation started as just a few towns on the coastline of the Atlantic Ocean. As new towns grew to the west of the coast, there was a need to move people and goods to such places as Buffalo, New York, or Pittsburgh, Pennsylvania. For a time, between 1825 and 1840, states dug canals to connect rivers near these towns. A canal is a waterway dug across land. But even the canals could not keep up with the country's transportation needs. U.S. citizens and immigrants from other countries were moving farther west to such regions as Kansas, Nebraska, Oregon, and California. These people walked alongside covered wagons filled with their belongings. They traveled for weeks through rainstorms and blistering heat.

It was the steam engine that gave the United States the transportation system it needed. Inventors in England and the United States came up with many ideas to use the steam engine to move people and goods faster. By 1869, railroad tracks crossed the continent. However, railroad companies built their tracks across American Indian land. American Indians were the first people to live in North America. As settlers built towns by the tracks, the railroads destroyed herds of buffalo, which many American Indians needed to survive. By 1890, thousands of American Indians had died, and their traditional way of life was destroyed.

THE FIRST TRAINS

The very first railroads in the United States used horses for power. The animals pulled wagons loaded with coal and stone along wooden tracks. The tracks ran just a short distance, for example from the side of a mountain to the bank of a river. In the early 1800s, U.S. citizens heard about experiments in England using steam engines.

In England, inventors found a way to move a railroad car by using the power of steam. In 1804, Englishman Richard Trevithick built the first train powered by a steam engine, called a locomotive. Trevithick used the locomotive to pull a load of iron ore about 9 miles (14.4 kilometers). English inventors continued to improve the locomotive. By 1825, an English inventor, George Stephenson, built a train that pulled fourteen wagons loaded with coal, flour, and passengers. People began calling the locomotive an iron horse.

Tom Thumb's race

Across the Atlantic Ocean, inventors in the United States worked on steam engines, too. A man named Peter Cooper built a small steam locomotive and called it *Tom Thumb.* At top speed, it pulled a railroad car 18 miles (28.8 kilometers) an hour. It was the first locomotive built in the U.S. to pull a load of passengers over public railroad tracks. Steam engines were exciting, but could they really pull a train faster than horses? In the summer of 1830, a driver of a horse-drawn coach challenged Cooper to a 7-mile (11.2-kilometer) race from Relay to Baltimore, Maryland. Burning wood to make steam, Cooper fired up the engine and brought *Tom Thumb* into the lead. Then the fan belt slipped and the engine died down. The horse won the race, but many people were impressed with the power of the locomotive.

EARLY ENGINES
1705 Thomas Newcomen's (English) steam engine pumps water from coal mines.
1782 James Watt's (Scottish) steam engine turns a crank connected to a wheel.
1805 Richard Trevithick (English) builds the first steam locomotive to ride on tracks.
1825 John Stevens (United States) builds the first steam locomotive in the U.S.
1829 Horatio Allen (United States) drives the *Stourbridge Lion,* the first steam locomotive to run on a public track in the U.S.

▼ The *Best Friend of Charleston* was the first train in the United States with regular passenger and freight service. It ran in Charleston, South Carolina, for six months in 1831. Then one day a fireman on the train heard steam escaping from the engine. To quiet it, he tied down a safety valve. The engine exploded.

▼ U.S. citizens were proud to watch the *Stourbridge Lion* arrive in Honesdale, Pennsylvania, in 1829. The locomotive was made in England. The Delaware and Hudson Canal Company bought the locomotive to run from a coal mine to their canal.

When the locomotive arrived, company officials were shocked to find that it weighed seven tons. They took a risk and let it travel on a 30-foot (9-meter) high wooden trestle across the Lackawaxen Creek. The locomotive crossed the swaying bridge without an accident. But the officials never let it run again.

MAKING STEAM

Steam engines combine fire and water to make steam.

1. Early engines burned wood. Later engines burned coal. Workers shoveled wood or coal into a firebox.

2. Heat from the firebox traveled in metal pipes to a closed container called a boiler. The boiler was filled with water.

3. As the water heated, it boiled and created steam.

4. The steam created pressure that, by a system of pistons and rods, moved the wheels of the train.

RAILROAD FEVER

By the 1830s, factory workers in the East were producing large quantities of cloth, glass, and iron. Miners were digging up coal. Thousands of immigrants from other countries came to the United States to find jobs in the factories and mines. Towns grew into busy cities.

As the nation grew, settlers started moving west to less crowded places. By the 1840s, thousands were moving all the way to Oregon and California. As distances to travel increased, so did the need for better transportation. Factories had to send their products to markets. Farmers had to send their crops to cities. People wanted to travel across the country faster than a horse and wagon could take them. Some businesspeople started forming railroad companies. These companies invested a great deal of money building bigger and better locomotives and thousands of miles of tracks. By 1840, there were almost 3,000 miles (4,800 kilometers) of track. All 26 states had railroads.

MILES OF TRACK
Railroad tracks in the United States grew rapidly until 1916. This list tells the total miles (kilometers) of tracks in various years:
1830 23 (36.8)
1840 2,818 (4,510)
1850 9,021 (14,435)
1860 30,626 (49,000)
1880 93,000 (148,800)
1916 254,000 (406,400)
2000 138,666 (221,865)

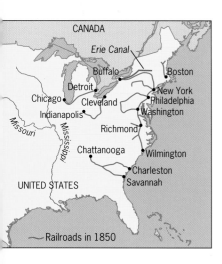

▲ In 1850, some railroad lines connected large cities to one another. Others connected cities to other means of transportation on oceans, rivers, and canals.

▼ This is a poster for a railroad in the 1840s. It tells when trains arrived and departed.

While many people in the North worked in factories and mines, most people in the South were farmers. In 1850, the South grew more than 80 percent of the world's cotton. With fewer people and factories, the South had less need for railroads than the North. Steamboats took cotton to Cincinnati, Ohio. From there, trains carried it to cities in the East. In 1850, there were railroads between such southern cities as Savannah and Atlanta, Georgia.

The first tracks

The railroad companies started with small strips of track. Some tracks ran from coal or iron mines to canals and rivers, where boats took the freight farther away. Other lines led from factory towns to larger cities. In 1835, Boston and Philadelphia were centers of the nation's railroads. Most of the lines covered no more than 45 miles (72 kilometers).

In 1834, the Allegheny Portage Railroad covered 345 miles (552 kilometers) through the steep Allegheny Mountains to connect Philadelphia and Pittsburgh, Pennsylvania. For part of the trip, freight and passengers were unloaded from the train and sent by boat on a canal. Then they boarded another train. This trip took almost four days, which was seventeen days shorter than the trip by wagon.

▼ A train pulls up next to a cloth factory in Manchester, New Hampshire. By 1850, locomotives had a funnel-shaped smokestack. This kept sparks from showering out onto the grass and starting fires. A wedge-shaped cowcatcher was attached to the front of the train. If an animal stood on the tracks, the cowcatcher prevented it from getting caught under the train wheels.

TRAINS AND TRACKS

In 1857, there were 51,000 miles (81,600 kilometers) of railroad tracks in the world. Almost half of them were in the United States. The growing railroad business provided hundreds of jobs. Workers were needed to build trains, to lay tracks, and to keep the trains moving.

Trains traveled from city to city. Between the cities, there were hills, mountains, forests, and rivers. They were not easy places to lay railroad tracks. Some workers were surveyors. They hiked through the woods and mountains to choose a route for the railroad. Then workers called graders started digging out the road to make it level for the tracks.

One of the hardest jobs was laying the tracks. First, workers set pieces of wood, called ties, in the ground. Then they lay iron rails on top of the ties. With heavy sledgehammers, they pounded metal spikes into the rails to keep the rails in place. Workers blasted tunnels through the mountains. They built bridges over rivers. If the land was flat, workers could lay 4 miles (6.4 kilometers) of track a day.

Working on the trains

Railroad workers had exciting but dangerous jobs. The engineer sat high in the cab of the locomotive and drove the train down the tracks. He blasted the train whistle if he saw animals on the track or when the train approached a town. The fireman stood by the engineer, shoveling wood or coal to make steam.

The flagman stood in the caboose, the last car on the train. If the train broke down, he walked down the tracks waving a flag or lantern to warn the next train to stop. Brakemen stood on top of the train and turned the brake wheels to stop the train. The switchmen had to go between the train cars and hitch or unhitch them. Sometimes they did this when the train was moving.

▶ This train was called *The Pioneer*. It was the first locomotive used in California, in 1852. The fireman stood by the pile of wood that burned in the engine. The engineer looked out the window. The smokestack on this locomotive was so wide and trunk-like that people nicknamed it "the Elephant."

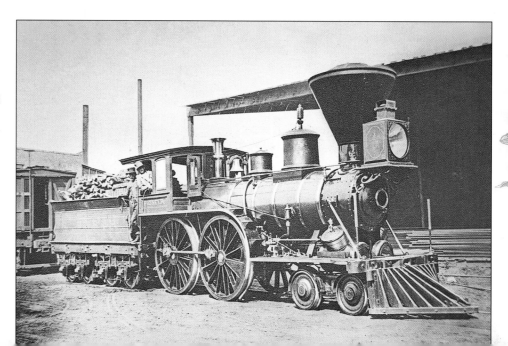

TELEGRAPHS AND TRAINS
Long before telephones and computers, Samuel Morse invented the telegraph. He sent coded messages of dots and dashes over telegraph wires. In the 1850s, railroad agents started sending telegraph messages to tell engineers when other trains were late or stalled on the tracks. This helped trains avoid hitting each other.

◄ By 1832, U.S. factories were building trains. Here, in the background, a boiler is lowered onto an engine. In front, a new engine has a headlight lit by a kerosene lamp. In 1881, electric headlights were introduced.

SAVE TIME AND MONEY
Compared to horses and boats, trains carried goods and people faster and for less money. For example:
• A trip from Cincinnati, Ohio, to St. Louis, Missouri, by steamboat took 70 hours. It took 16 hours by train.
• It cost 50 cents to mail a letter in 1815. The cost in 1850 was 3 cents.

TRACKS TO THE WEST

From 1840 to 1860, the nation's population grew from 17.1 million to 31.4 million. The number of states grew from 26 to 33. More people lived west of the Mississippi River than ever before. At first, most people lived on farms that were far from each other and miles from small towns.

Railroad companies could not afford to build tracks to these small towns. In 1850, the U.S. government offered to help. It gave away thousands of acres of land to the railroad companies. (An acre is an area about 70 yards (64 meters) square.) The companies built railroad tracks and stations. They also raised money by selling some of the land to settlers.

This plan helped the railroads and settlers, but it hurt the American Indians who lived on the land. Years earlier, the government had forced many tribes to move to this land from the East. The government had promised that this western land would be the Indians' new home forever. But railroad companies and settlers would take it.

▼ The railroad station is a busy place. Some people wait excitedly to pick up special packages and passengers. Others arrive by stagecoach to board the train.

Small towns had small stations with just a few benches. Stations in larger cities had big waiting rooms and restaurants. The tall building with the pointed roof is a water tower. A railroad worker will use the water to fill the boiler of the locomotive.

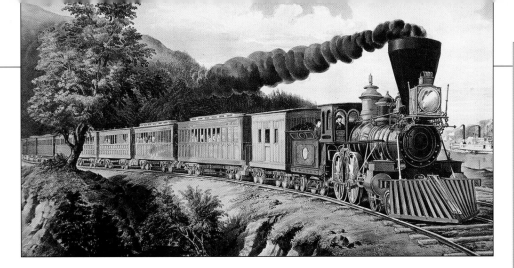

Railroad companies painted their locomotives shiny black. Some added red and gold designs to it. People were fascinated by the sight of a powerful locomotive with its long trail of smoke.

Unwanted competition

The railroad hurt some businesses, especially those that earned money by transporting people by wagons, stagecoaches, and boats. In 1856, the Chicago and Rock Island Railroad built the first bridge across the Mississippi River. Ferryboat owners were furious. Would people need ferryboats if they could ride a train across the river? One day a boat rammed the bridge, causing a fire that burned down the bridge. The boat owner blamed the railroad company for putting up the bridge. Abraham Lincoln, the lawyer for the railroad company, convinced the court that the railroad had a right to build the bridge.

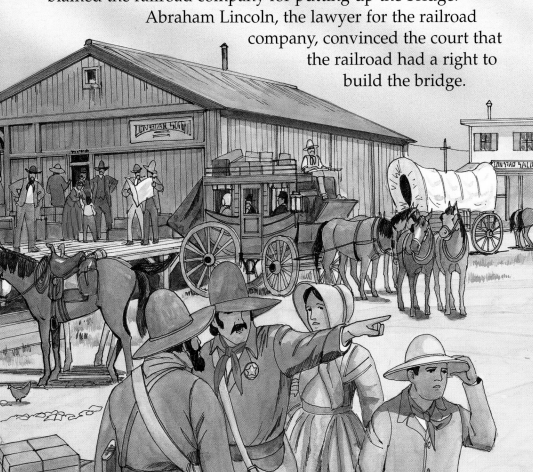

THE CIVIL WAR

By 1861, the United States faced a serious problem. Eleven states in the South decided to leave the nation and form their own Confederate States of America. They claimed that people in the South had different needs from people in the North. Among other things, southern states supported slavery and were angry that the U.S. government wanted all new states to outlaw slavery.

In April 1861, the Confederate army fired cannons on Fort Sumter, a U.S. fort in South Carolina. This was the start of the Civil War. It was hard to believe that Americans would fight a war against each other. Most people expected such a war to last just a few weeks. But it lasted four years. During that period, more than 2 million soldiers fought for the Union army. About 800,000 fought for the Confederates. More U.S. soldiers died in that war than in any other war in U.S. history. In a single, one-day battle, 4,700 soldiers died.

More than 20 major battles took place during the Civil War. Most of them took place in the southern states. In the end, the Union army won the war. It was able to use a much bigger railroad system than the Confederate army. The railroads took cannons, horses, wagons, and thousands of soldiers to the southern battle sites. They also carried food, water, and ammunition for the soldiers.

STOLEN WAR TRAIN
In April 1862, a southern passenger train picked up four men at a station in Georgia. The men told the train conductor that they were volunteers for the Confederate army. Actually the men were Union supporters. While the passengers and crew got off the train to eat breakfast, the men stole the train. After a few miles, they stopped and tore up the tracks behind them.

▶ This is a Union depot and supply station in the North. Soldiers will board the trains while food, guns, and animals are loaded onto the freight cars.

14

THE HOMESTEAD ACT
In 1862, the U.S. Congress passed the Homestead Act. It gave 160 acres (65 hectares – about the size of 70 soccer fields) to any settler who paid a small fee and agreed to work the land for five years. The Act provided homes for 600,000 settlers. The nation's population spread westward.

▼ On November 15, 1864, General Sherman's troops set Atlanta on fire. They burned homes, farms, businesses, and anything that might help the South survive. Sherman ordered his soldiers to rip up the railroad tracks. On April 9, 1865, the Confederates surrendered.

Railroads in the South
Because the South had fewer factories and people, its railroads were not as advanced as the North's. Armies on both sides fiercely tried to protect their own tracks and trains and destroy the enemy's. Soldiers ripped up tracks and burned them until the rails could be bent around trees. Repair workers constantly rebuilt tracks and bridges. The Union's famous General Sherman wrote that his 300-mile (480-kilometer) march that nearly destroyed Georgia would have been impossible without the railroads bringing his army fresh supplies each day.

15

CROSSING THE CONTINENT

Even while the Civil War continued, President Abraham Lincoln and Congress made plans for uniting the nation. They not only wanted to reunite northern and southern states under one government. They also wanted to unite the eastern states to the western states by railroad.

In the 1850s, a man named Theodore Judah traveled twice from California to Washington, D.C. He tried to convince Congress to help build a transcontinental railroad from California to existing railroad tracks in the East. It took about twelve years for Congress to agree to the idea.

By 1862, the population had spread across the continent to the Pacific Coast. Railroads in the East were proving that trains could ship products faster and cheaper than wagons. In 1862, President Lincoln signed the Pacific Railroad Act. The government agreed to give two railroad companies land and money to build a railroad and telegraph line across the continent. The companies would get varying amounts of money depending on the difficulty of laying the tracks.

The Central Pacific and Union Pacific
Judah returned to California to make a plan for the Central Pacific Railroad. Its tracks would start in Sacramento and head eastward. He convinced four wealthy business owners to invest money in the Central Pacific. They were Leland Stanford, a grocer; Charles Crocker, a merchant; and Mark Hopkins and Collis P. Huntington, partners in a hardware store. Judah died in 1863 and the Big Four, as the wealthy men were called, led the Central Pacific project. Meanwhile, the Union Pacific Railroad made plans to lay tracks westward from Omaha, Nebraska. Thomas Durant and Grenville M. Dodge made many of its decisions.

▼ States in the North and South wanted the tracks through their land. Finally, a route from Sacramento to Omaha was chosen. Railroad companies were paid from $16,000 a mile (1.6 kilometers) to put tracks over flat land to $48,000 a mile for tracks through high mountains.

FROM THE EAST TO CALIFORNIA
There were several ways to travel to California:
• Horse or mule-drawn wagons traveled from Missouri (journey time 6 to 8 months).
• Ships from New York sailed around South America (9 to 12 months).
• Ships from New York sailed to the Isthmus of Panama. People crossed Panama by canoes and mules. Then they boarded other ships to California (3 to 5 months).

ONE OF THE BIG FOUR
The "Big Four" investors had to raise millions of dollars to build the railroad. In 1861, Leland Stanford was elected governor of California. Thanks to him, the state government gave land and money to build the railroad. After serving as governor, Stanford owned construction companies that built the railroad. He became a rich man. In 1884, he founded Stanford University.

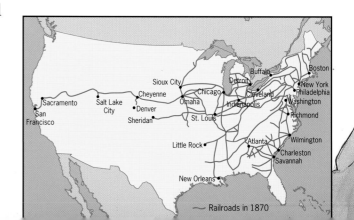

Railroads in 1870

▶ In this photo from 1868, officials of the Union Pacific Railroad hold a meeting in a private car of a train. Thomas Durant sits third from the left at the table.

▼ **Surveyors** scramble through western mountains to mark the route of the tracks. Slowly and carefully, they passed tools and instruments to each other. Below, a locomotive at the end of the tracks brings railroad officials to inspect the work.

17

BUILDING FROM THE WEST

The job was enormous! The transcontinental railroad would be more than twice as long as any other railroad in the world. Workers would have to build through deserts, prairies, the Sierra Nevada, the Rocky Mountains, and the homelands of several tribes of American Indians.

Workers on the Central Pacific Railroad started work on January 8, 1863. Their job seemed impossible. They had to lay tracks through the rocky cliffs of the Sierra Nevada. Workers used 500 kegs of explosives a day to blast away at the solid rock. Day after day, they blasted, then dug, then picked away with hand tools. When they reached deep canyons, they bolted together high wooden trestle bridges.

The mountains were only part of the workers' problems. Blizzards covered the tracks and sometimes buried men alive. It took four years to dig 15 tunnels, build miles of trestle bridges, and lay 125 miles (200 kilometers) of track through the Sierra Nevada. The workers finally reached the California-Nevada border. Then they had to cross the state of Nevada.

GETTING SUPPLIES
The western forests supplied plenty of trees to make railroad ties. Everything else had to be shipped from the East. Ships carried locomotives, cars, shovels, hammers, spikes, and rails around South America to San Francisco.

As tracks were built in California, locomotives hauled the supplies out to the workers. Because the government needed the same materials for the Civil War, supplies were scarce and more expensive until 1865.

▼ Rail by rail, the Central Pacific workers built 689 miles (1,000 kilometers) of railroad. Union Pacific workers built 1,086 miles (1,735 kilometers) over much flatter land.

18

Workers needed

Charles Crocker was in charge of hiring railroad workers. He needed thousands. The West did not have a large workforce. Many men preferred working in the silver mines of Nevada with hopes of getting rich quickly. Crocker finally went to San Francisco's Chinatown to offer jobs to Chinese men. These men had come to California in the gold rush, which ended by 1859. Now they needed jobs. Crocker sent agents to China to hire more men. The railroad paid for their transportation, but the Chinese had to repay the money with interest. In all, Crocker hired 12,000 Chinese workers.

Heroes of the railroad

The Central Pacific Railroad would never have been built without the Chinese workers. Although they spoke little English, they quickly learned the job. Sometimes their bosses gave them very dangerous jobs. For one job, they were lowered in a basket over a high cliff. While the basket swayed, they pounded holes in the cliff and lit explosives.

The Chinese did difficult and dangerous work, but were not always treated well. They had to pay for their food and beds inside the workers' railroad car. Other workers did not have to pay.

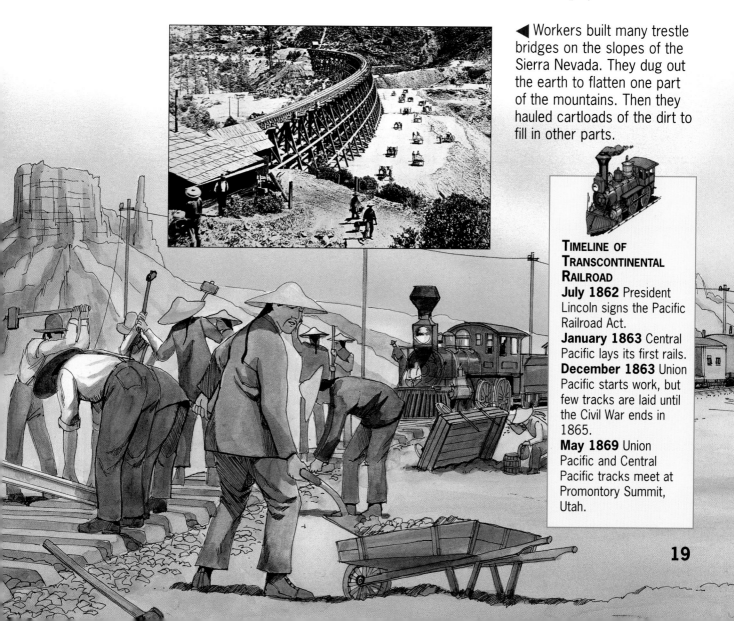

◀ Workers built many trestle bridges on the slopes of the Sierra Nevada. They dug out the earth to flatten one part of the mountains. Then they hauled cartloads of the dirt to fill in other parts.

TIMELINE OF TRANSCONTINENTAL RAILROAD
July 1862 President Lincoln signs the Pacific Railroad Act.
January 1863 Central Pacific lays its first rails.
December 1863 Union Pacific starts work, but few tracks are laid until the Civil War ends in 1865.
May 1869 Union Pacific and Central Pacific tracks meet at Promontory Summit, Utah.

BUILDING FROM THE EAST

The Union Pacific had its own problems. There were few trees in the flat plains of Nebraska. Boats on the Missouri River carried wooden ties, iron rails, and parts of trains from eastern towns. Then horses hauled the supplies to the work site. Forty wagonloads of supplies were needed every day.

Work started in December 1863, in the middle of the Civil War. But barely 40 miles (64 kilometers) of tracks were laid by May 1866. There were few workers because men were fighting the war. Supplies and tools were just as scarce. After the war, the Union Pacific increased production. Thousands of soldiers became railroad workers. Army generals became their bosses.

Many of the workers were immigrants from Ireland. They had left their country to escape hunger and unemployment. The Union Pacific welcomed them. Former General John Casement and his brother, Dan, were in charge of Union Pacific workers. Speed was the most important thing to them. In 1866, their workers completed 266 miles (425 kilometers) of track. Workers hauled and hammered away through freezing winter snowstorms and violent prairie thunderstorms. In the winter of 1866–1867, the Missouri River froze so thickly that workers built temporary tracks on it and sent over their supplies by train.

Mountains ahead

The Union Pacific workers crossed Nebraska and Wyoming into eastern Utah, laying up to 6 miles (9.6 kilometers) of track per day. Then they faced the Rocky Mountains in the fall of 1867. Just as the Central Pacific workers did in the Sierra Nevada, work crews dug tunnels through the mountains. They reached the other side near the Great Salt Lake. Central Pacific workers were just a few miles away.

THE WORK TRAIN
Wherever the crew laid tracks, the work train pulled up nearby. This train was like a town on wheels. It had bunk cars where 300 people slept, a dining car with a long table down the center, a general store, a blacksmith shop, and a car to carry the rails and spikes. Cattle, needed to feed the crew, grazed beside the work train.

AMERICAN INDIANS
In Nebraska and Wyoming, the crew laid tracks right through the hunting grounds of the Sioux and Cheyenne tribes. To try to protect their homeland, the American Indians ripped up telegraph wires, set fires, and attacked crews. Eventually 5,000 U.S. soldiers arrived to protect the tracks and crews.

▶ Union Pacific Railroad workers stand in front of a construction train in1868. Brakemen stand on top of the cars.

▼ Bridge-builders bolted together tons of wood to build trestle bridges across rivers, creeks, and canyons. Workers cut down trees in Minnesota. They floated the logs down the Mississippi River and sent them by boat up the Missouri River to Omaha. Horses and mules carted the wood to the bridge site.

Crocker's bet

By the spring of 1868, the two railroad companies raced to lay down tracks. Every mile they covered meant more money and land for the company owners. When Charles Crocker of the Central Pacific heard that Union Pacific crews laid 8 1/2 miles (13.6 kilometers) of track in a day, he bet $10,000 that his crew could lay 10 miles (16 kilometers) in a day. To everyone's surprise, Crocker won the bet. That record for track-laying has never been broken.

21

PROMONTORY SUMMIT

By March 1869, both railroad companies had reached Utah, working at incredible speed. Since the government was paying them thousands of dollars a mile, neither company wanted to stop. No one had yet chosen a stopping point.

In April, the grading crew of the Union Pacific passed the grading crew of the Central Pacific. The crews leveled 258 miles (413 kilometers) of extra land. Finally on April 9, officials from both railroads decided to have the tracks meet at Promontory Summit in Utah. Congress agreed. On May 1, the Central Pacific crew laid their last rail. On May 7, the Union Pacific crew did the same. An empty space the size of two rails separated the two tracks.

On May 7, California's Governor Stanford, along with other government and railroad officials, arrived by train. By now Stanford was also president of Central Pacific. Thomas Durant, vice-president of Union Pacific, was expected to arrive that day, too. But his train was stopped in Wyoming by a crew of railroad workers who had not been paid. Durant arranged for the payment, and the workers let the train pass. It arrived in Promontory on May 10, the day of the ceremony.

The ceremony

At least twenty newspaper reporters and a crowd of 500 people watched the ceremony. Chinese workers from the Central Pacific and Irish workers from the Union Pacific set in place a special railroad tie made from a California laurel tree. The tie was wrapped in silver and had the date inscribed on it. Then the last rail was placed, and the crowd was silenced. There were many special spikes, donated from several states. Some were silver, others iron covered with gold. Railroad officials made speeches as they pounded in the special spikes. Most reports say that Leland Stanford had the honor of hitting the last spike—named the Golden Spike— with a silver hammer. The spike was wired to telegraph lines so that telegraph offices around the nation could hear the sound.

THE HUMAN COSTS
Hundreds of human lives were lost during the building of the railroad. Many workers died from accidents on steep cliffs and over deep canyons. Many died of disease during the freezing winters. Railroad workers and American Indians also died while fighting over the right to be on the land.

▼ Reporters said that Stanford swung but missed the Golden Spike. But the telegraph operator faked the noise of the hammer and tapped out the word "done." The news flashed throughout the country. To celebrate, fireworks were set off in Chicago and a 100-gun salute was fired in New York City. The Liberty Bell was rung in Philadelphia, and a glowing ball was dropped from the Capitol Building in Washington, D.C.

THE GOLDEN SPIKE

The famous Golden Spike was a gift from a wealthy San Francisco man named David Hewes. Along with the date and names of railroad officials, these words were printed on the spike: "May God continue the unity of our Country as this Railroad unites the two great Oceans of the world".

▲ After Stanford hit the Golden Spike, Union Pacific's engine *119* and Central Pacific's *Jupiter* inched toward each other until they touched. Officials broke champagne bottles while the crowd cheered. Later, workers replaced the special spikes and tie with ordinary ones. The Golden Spike and silver hammer are now part of an art collection at Stanford University. The laurel tie was returned to San Francisco, but burned in a fire during the earthquake of 1906. The men shaking hands in this photograph are Sam Montague, chief engineer of the Central Pacific (left) and Grenville Dodge, chief engineer of the Union Pacific.

RAILROADS BRING CHANGE

In 1870, the nation had 52,922 miles (84,675 kilometers) of track. And the railroads kept building. By 1890, there were 163,597 miles (261,755 kilometers) of track, enough to circle the world six times. There were five transcontinental railroads. A cross-country trip took ten days. A first-class ticket cost $136 (worth about $1,800 today).

Railroads allowed U.S. citizens to move their products faster across the country. Farmers in Nebraska and Dakota shipped their wheat to eastern cities. Ranchers in Texas and Wyoming sent their cattle east to slaughterhouses and meat-packing companies. Towns quickly grew along the railroads.

Broken promises

For many years, the U.S. government had treaties with American Indian leaders. These were promises that the American Indians could keep some parts of the western land and the government would own other parts. By the 1860s, the government ignored the treaties and let the railroad companies build through the Indian lands. Eventually, the Indian homeland was overtaken by the settlement and development the railroads helped bring. Railroad passengers killed many buffalo, often just for sport. This was different from the Indians, for whom the buffalo was the main source of food, shelter, and clothing. Many Indians had been moved to reservations set up by the government. But with the great changes brought by the railroads, the remaining Indians not on reservations eventually also had to move to reservations.

GREAT INDIAN LEADERS
Chief Joseph, leader of the Nez Perce, fought until 1877 for his people's land in the Northwest.
Sitting Bull, a Sioux leader, defended his people's land in Dakota until 1881.
Geronimo was the Apache leader in 1886, when the U.S. Army forced them off their land in the Southwest.

▶ The Illinois Central Railroad used this advertisement to attract customers in 1886. The railroad's first route crossed the state of Illinois. Later, its trains went to the South and the West. The railroad is still in business.

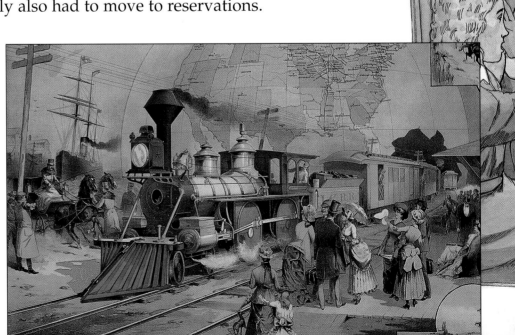

24

Time zones

Before 1883, towns set their clocks by looking at the sun. A clock in St. Louis might say 2:00 while a clock in Chicago might say 2:05. It was hard to know what time a train would arrive. This made it difficult for passengers to catch the train and for repair workers to complete their work before a train arrived. In 1883, the country was divided into four time zones. Moving west, the time in each zone was exactly one hour earlier. Railroad companies started to print accurate train schedules.

▼ From 1872 to 1876, settlers and travelers from the East killed four million buffalo. Some did it just for fun. Others sold the meat to railroad companies to feed the workers. Bones were sold to factories in the East.

BETTER RAILROADS

Here are some of the improvements in railroads in the 1880s:
- Steel rails replaced wooden rails.
- Air brakes replaced brakemen who stood on top of each car.
- Two sets of parallel tracks replaced the need for two trains to travel in opposite directions on the same track. (One train waited until another train completed its run.)
- The first trains traveled at about 12 miles (19 kilometers) per hour. In 1893, a speed record was set at 112.5 miles (180 kilometers) per hour.

FILLING THE CONTINENT

Between 1870 and 1890, nearly ten million people moved west of the Mississippi River. Many of these people had already moved westward across the country several times. Each time, they started a new life in hope of more land and happiness than they had before.

Western land had great appeal to immigrants— people who moved to the United States from other countries. Millions of people from Germany, Russia, and eastern Europe left their countries because they were being punished for their religious or political beliefs. In the United States, these people enjoyed freedom. In addition, in the West they could become landowners. Railroad companies encouraged settlers to live in the West by advertising in newspapers all over the world. The ads bragged about cheap land and rich soil on the Great Plains. Some companies offered free train tickets to the West.

Railroads would make money later by shipping goods to and from the western settlers.

▼ In 1875, the Northern Pacific Railroad advertised land in Montana and Dakota Territories. In 1889, Dakota Territory was made into two states: North Dakota and South Dakota.

Living on the Plains

Many settlers struggled with their new lives in the West. The ads did not mention that the Great Plains had blazing hot summers that could turn fields to dust. Insects could destroy crops. Rains could flood the fields. Windstorms could blow animals across a farmyard. Many settlers sold their land back to the railroad companies and moved farther west. Others stayed through the bad times and enjoyed better times later.

American Indians generally did not enjoy better times. Some Indians worked on the railroads. But most were forced by the U.S. government to move to reservations. With railroads linking east and west, settlers from the East quickly and greatly increased, and American Indians' traditional ways of life ended.

THE LAST OPEN LAND

During the 1800s, present-day Oklahoma was called Indian Territory. The U.S. government kept the land for American Indians and settlers took over the rest of the West. By 1890, settlers wanted more land. The government opened Indian Territory to settlers, too. By 1893, almost all American Indian tribes lived on government reservations.

RAILROAD UPDATE

The first trip from New York to California took ten days. Passengers changed trains in Chicago, Omaha, and Promontory. In 1934, a Union Pacific train made the trip in just under 57 hours. By then, trains were sleek, silver "streamliners." They had diesel engines that burned oil using the heat from hot, compressed (squeezed) air.

▼ New settlers arrive with their belongings at a railroad station in the Great Plains. Towns quickly grew along the railroads. Between 1870 and 1890, the population of Kansas City grew from 3,000 to 37,000. Omaha's population grew from 16,000 to 140,000.

HISTORICAL MAP OF THE UNITED STATES

By 1890, the United States stretched from coast to coast. There were 44 states. Nearly 164,000 miles (262,400 kilometers) of railroad track connected cities and towns across the nation. By 1893, five transcontinental railroads crossed the country. The Northern Pacific and Great Northern crossed through such northern states as Montana and Washington. The Southern Pacific crossed through Texas and Arizona. By 1893, almost all American Indian tribes lived on government reservations.

River
Railroads in 1890
Indian reservations in 1880
Transcontinental Railroad

HAWAIIAN ISLANDS

0	250	500 miles
0	400	800 kilometers

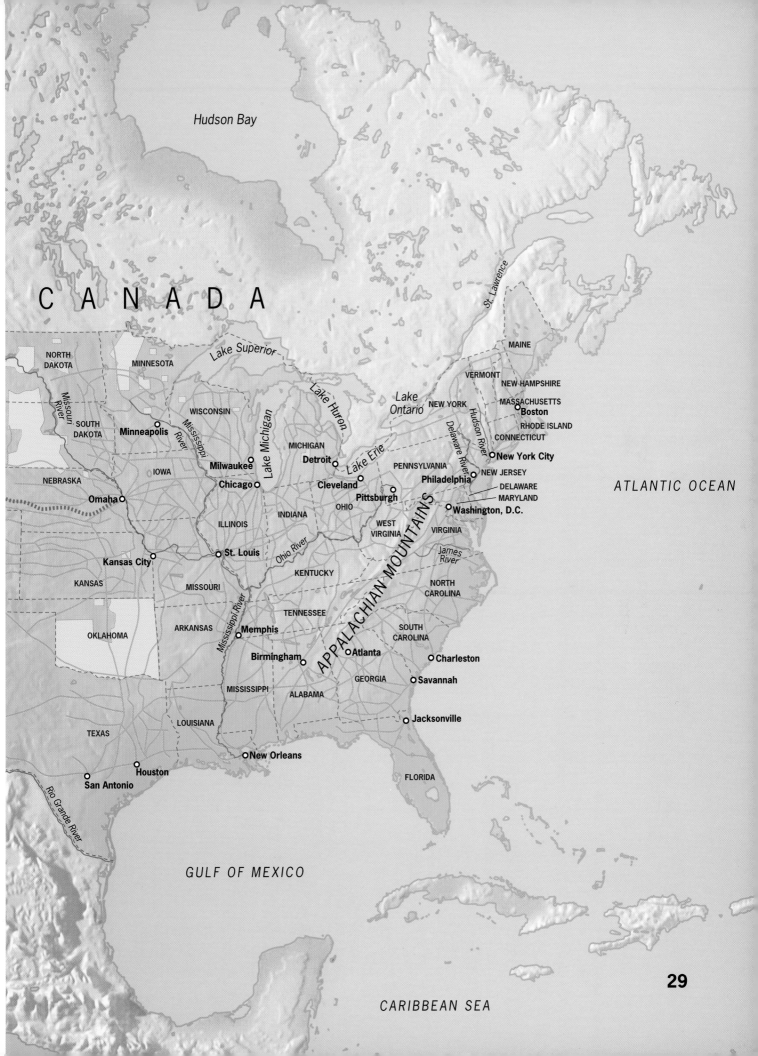

Hudson Bay

CANADA

NORTH DAKOTA

MINNESOTA

Lake Superior

MAINE

VERMONT

NEW HAMPSHIRE

SOUTH DAKOTA

Missouri River

WISCONSIN

Lake Huron

Lake Ontario

NEW YORK

MASSACHUSETTS

Boston

RHODE ISLAND

Minneapolis

Mississippi River

MICHIGAN

CONNECTICUT

Hudson River

NEBRASKA

IOWA

Milwaukee

Lake Michigan

Detroit

Lake Erie

PENNSYLVANIA

Delaware River

New York City

NEW JERSEY

Philadelphia

Chicago

Cleveland

Pittsburgh

DELAWARE

ATLANTIC OCEAN

Omaha

ILLINOIS

INDIANA

OHIO

MARYLAND

Washington, D.C.

WEST VIRGINIA

VIRGINIA

Kansas City

St. Louis

Ohio River

James River

KANSAS

MISSOURI

KENTUCKY

NORTH CAROLINA

APPALACHIAN MOUNTAINS

OKLAHOMA

ARKANSAS

Mississippi River

TENNESSEE

Memphis

SOUTH CAROLINA

Birmingham

Atlanta

Charleston

GEORGIA

Savannah

MISSISSIPPI

ALABAMA

TEXAS

LOUISIANA

Jacksonville

New Orleans

Houston

FLORIDA

San Antonio

Rio Grande River

St. Lawrence

GULF OF MEXICO

CARIBBEAN SEA

GLOSSARY

boiler closed container for making steam by heating water

brakeman person who makes the train stop

caboose usually the last car on a train

canal body of water made by people. A canal connects one body of water to another and is like a water highway.

Civil War in the United States, a war between the North and the South

Confederate referring to the southern states that left the United States during the Civil War

Congress branch of the U.S. government that makes laws

depot building used for railroad passengers or freight

engineer person who operates the locomotive on a train

fireman person who puts coal or wood into the locomotive's engine to make steam

flagman person who walks down the tracks and, by waving a flag, warns other trains about a stopped train

freight car railway carriage used for carrying goods

gold rush starting in 1849, the time when people rushed to California to find gold

grader railroad worker who makes the land level or flat so others can build tracks

Great Plains area of grassland east of the Rocky Mountains. North to south, it stretches 2,500 miles (4,020 kilometers) from Canada to Texas.

immigrant someone who moves from another country

interest money paid for the use of money

invest give money for something that is expected to provide income later

Isthmus of Panama narrow strip of land that connects the Atlantic and Pacific Oceans and connects North and South America

kerosene thick oily mixture made from petroleum. It is burned in lamps and stoves.

locomotive engine used to pull a train

Mormon member of the Church of Jesus Christ of Latter-day Saints. Many Mormons moved to present-day Utah in the 1850s to avoid criticism of, and attacks on, their religious beliefs.

rail piece of iron or steel laid across railroad ties to make tracks

rancher person who owns a ranch, a farm where horses, cattle, or sheep are raised

reservation area of land set aside by the U.S. government for American Indians to live

slaughterhouse place where animals are killed for food

spike large, strong nail

stagecoach boxlike car pulled by horses in which people traveled long distances

surrender give up or admit you cannot win a battle

surveyor person who looks at and measures land for the purpose of setting boundaries or planning to build something

switchman person who connects two railroad cars together

telegraph machine that sends messages in the form of a code through electrical wires

tie one of many pieces of wood that are set about 12 inches (30 centimeters) apart to make a railroad track

transcontinental railroad train tracks going across a continent

treaty written agreement, usually between two nations

trestle framework of wood or metal used as a bridge to support railroad tracks or a road

Union northern states that supported the U.S. government during the Civil War

30

TIMELINE OF EVENTS IN THIS BOOK

1705 In England, Thomas Newcomen's steam engine pumps water from coal mines

1825 John Stevens builds the first steam locomotive that runs on tracks in the United States

1829 The *Stourbridge Lion* arrives in New York from England, the first steam locomotive to run on a public track in the United States

1830 Peter Cooper's *Tom Thumb* locomotive races a horse-drawn wagon

1844 Samuel Morse transmits the first practical telegraph service in the United States from Washington, D.C., to Baltimore, Maryland

1845 Texas joins the United States

1848 As a result of the Mexican War, the United States gains California, Nevada, Utah, and parts of Wyoming, New Mexico, Colorado, and Arizona

1848 The gold rush begins as gold is discovered near Sacramento, California

1853 In the Gadsden Purchase, the United States buys southern Arizona and New Mexico from Mexico

1854 The Chicago and Rock Island Railroad is the first train to reach the Mississippi River from the East

1854 Theodore Judah builds a railroad in California that is 21 miles (33.6 kilometers) long, from Sacramento to the gold fields in the Sierra Nevada

1856 The Chicago and Rock Island Railroad builds a railroad bridge over the Mississippi River. It runs between Rock Island, Illinois, and Davenport, Iowa.

1861 to 1865 Northern and southern states fight the Civil War

1862 President Abraham Lincoln signs the Pacific Railway Act. It provides money to build the first transcontinental railroad in the United States.

1862 Congress passes the Homestead Act, giving land to settlers in the West

1863 to 1869 The Union Pacific and Central Pacific Railroads build the first transcontinental railroad

1864 George Pullman builds the first railroad car designed for sleeping

1883 The United States is divided into four standard time zones

1889 The first land rush in Oklahoma takes place. The U.S. government allows settlers to claim land that had been given to American Indians.

FURTHER READING

Blashfield, Jean F. *The Transcontinental Railroad.* Minneapolis, Minn.: Compass Point Books, 2001.

Evans, Clark J. *The Central Pacific Railroad.* Danbury, Conn.: Scholastic Library Publishing, 2003.

Halpern, Monica. *Building the Transcontinental Roilroad.* Washington, D.C.: National Geographic Society, 2002.

Levinson, Nancy. *Women and the Railroads.* New York: Penguin Putnam Books for Young Readers, 2000.

Magram, Hannah Straus. *Railroads of the West.* Broomall, Penn.: Mason Crest, 2002.

Ray, Kurt. *New Roads, Canals, and Railroads in Early 19th-Century America: The Transportation Revolution.* New York: Rosen Publishing, 2003.

Spangenburg, Ray, and Diane Moser. *The Story of America's Railroads.* Bridgewater, N.J.: Replica Books, 1999.

Uschan, Michael V. *The Transcontinental Roilroad.* Milwaukee, Wisc.: Gareth Stevens, 2003.

PLACES TO VISIT

Allegheny Portage Railroad National Historic Site
110 Federal Park Road
Gallitzin, PA 16641
Telephone: (814) 886-6150

B. & O. Railroad Museum
901 W. Pratt Street
Baltimore, MD 21223
Telephone: (410) 752-2490

California State Railroad Museum
111 "I" Street
Sacramento, CA 95814
Telephone: (916) 445-6645

Golden Spike National Historic Site
P.O. Box 897
Brigham City, UT 84302
Telephone: (435) 471-2209

INDEX